Anthony Quinn (1915–2001)

Anthony Quinn's Eye

A Lifetime of Creating and Collecting Art

Donald Kuspit

Jay Parini

Tom Roberts

Foreword by Katherine Quinn

Tribute by Kirk Douglas

BRISTOL HOUSE PRESS

in association with

W.W. Norton & Company

For Antonia and Ryan

Anthony at age thirteen, 1928

Anthony Quinn's Eye

A Lifetime of Creating and Collecting Art

Essays by Donald Kuspit, Jay Parini, Tom Roberts

Vignettes about Anthony Quinn's life by Katherine Quinn

Copyright © 2004 by Bristol House Press

All images are from the collection of the estate of Anthony Quinn

All rights reserved. No part of the contents of this book may be reproduced without the written permission of the publisher.

Printed and bound in the United States of America

1 2 3 4 5 6 7 8 9 0

First Edition

ISBN 0-393-06008-X

Limited Edition: ISBN 0-393-06009-8

Library of Congress Cataloging-in-Publication Data

Kuspit, Donald B. (Donald Burton), 1935-

Anthony Quinn's eye : a lifetime of creating and collecting art / Donald Kuspit, Jay Parini, Tom Roberts ; foreword by Katherine Quinn ; tribute by Kirk Douglas.— 1st ed.

    p. cm.

ISBN 0-393-06008-X — ISBN 0-393-06009-8 (deluxe limited ed.)

1. Quinn, Anthony, 1915- 2. Quinn, Anthony, 1915—Art collections.

I. Parini, Jay. II. Roberts, Tom, 1944- III. Title.

N6537.Q555A4 2004

709'.2—dc22

2004011458

Published in 2004 by Bristol House Press

PO Box 539, Bristol, Rhode Island 02809

www.BristolHousePress.com

Distributed by W.W. Norton & Company

500 Fifth Avenue, New York, New York 10110

www.wwnorton.com

W.W. Norton & Company Ltd.

Castle House, 75/76 Wells Street, London, W1T 3QT

Contents

8   Foreword

Katherine Quinn

20   His Mind, His Eye, and His Hand

Jay Parini

80   Making and Collecting Art

Donald Kuspit

212   A Tribute

Kirk Douglas

215   Acting

Tom Roberts

Foreword

Katherine Quinn

Anthony with daughter Antonia, wife Katherine, and son Ryan, 1999

The idea for this book started when a group of people interested in organizing an exhibition of my husband's artwork came to tour our estate in Bristol, Rhode Island. They brought with them a consultant, a man named Malcolm Grear, a world-renowned graphic designer. The group was clearly overwhelmed by the vast collection of sculptures, paintings, and drawings that Tony had created, so we discussed how to make a selection that would accurately represent the scope and scale of his work.

When asked his opinion, Malcolm said, "The exhibition would be lacking if it didn't include a representation of the objects Mr. Quinn collected as well as those objects he created." He explained that he was equally impressed with the books, eggs, masks, rocks, stones, artifacts, and paintings by other artists that were scattered throughout the house and barn. "The artist's eye is evident everywhere." The idea appealed to everyone, but the execution of such a visionary project was beyond the budget. A few weeks later, Malcolm reciprocated my tour of the estate and gave me and my two children—Antonia and Ryan—a tour of his studio. I was as impressed by his talent and creativity as he was by Tony's. I asked him if he would consider designing a book with me, based on his concept.

I have spent this past year relearning and appreciating the genius of the man I was lucky enough to call my husband. I knew Tony for sixteen years. The day we met, I knew that my life was changed forever. It was his piercing eyes that first struck me. He seemed to be evaluating me critically with one eye while welcoming me with the other—I wasn't sure if I was afraid or in love. Instead

of shaking my hand, he threw his arm around my neck and gave me a bear hug—I was in love.

We worked together for many years, and each day I learned something new—a knowledge that cannot be learned from books, only from participating in a life full of curiosity, hungry for knowledge, for discovery, for creating something original, never wanting to fall into pattern or cliché. Being around Tony, one couldn't help but be energized, feeling that anything was possible.

He was seventy when we met. Instead of resting on his accomplishments and retiring to a life of comfort and leisure, he was planning projects for the next twenty years. He was rehearsing a nine-month road tour of the stage production of *Zorba*, working on dozens of paintings at once, having sculptures cast at five different foundries (none alone was able to handle the volume of work he was creating), writing scripts and books, and searching for characters to play that would satisfy his driving, creative spirit.

Tony would receive endless invitations to travel, to be in the company of royals, famous actors, and notorious gangsters—his choice. But he preferred tackling a big blank canvas in his studio, riding his mountain bike through Central Park in search of new hills to conquer (he never traveled the mapped-out paths), sitting at a little Italian restaurant drinking espresso with his good friend Sam Shaw, or just walking along the East River and stopping to read a poem or play a game of chess with the men who sit at the little chess tables along the river walk.

Those were the times when he was happiest. He got energy from the people he met on his excursions. He shook hands, stopped,

PRECEDING PAGE Driveway, Bristol, Rhode Island

talked, learned—always seeking, always taking in the sights, the smells and the sounds of reality. It gave him fuel for his creations. The people around him were usually profoundly touched by meeting him—he gave back more energy than he took in, almost as if he absorbed it, multiplied it, and gave it back. I learned the power of one human being to change the lives of many. Yet he was humble and would not hesitate to write a fan letter to a fellow famous actor or director if he saw a performance that moved him.

Tony's connection with nature was just as vital to his creative hunger as was his connection with people. He chose to spend the last decade of his life in a natural environment, one distant from the pace and clutter of urban action—although the search for the perfect place was not an easy one. He knew he wanted to live in New England, but where? Where was there enough space for him to enjoy his privacy, be near the water, work on his paintings and sculpture, and still be near enough to civilization that he wouldn't feel lonely?

He asked Sotheby's for brochures of places with these criteria. He was sent hundreds. After sifting through—yes, no, yes, no—and narrowing the search to twenty or so, we set off from New York on a road trip with our then one-year-old daughter. It was one disappointment after another, with the last one being just down the road from the house we finally settled on. Thanksgiving weekend and nowhere else to go. We had lunch with a real estate agent who was determined to find Tony his dream house. "Mr. Quinn, what exactly are you looking for?" Without hesitating, he answered, "I want a ranch-style house, all on one level—I may not be able to

FOLLOWING PAGES House and studios, Bristol

climb stairs in ten years. It must be near the water, have plenty of land for my daughter to run around on, and, oh, it should have a barn big enough to store all of the artwork I've created and collected over the years—I love barns." The man's eyes lit up. "There's a house down the road from the one you just saw; it's exactly what you are describing—the owner put it on the market a few days ago." He tried to call, but no one was home. Tony said, "Let's just drive over and see it." As we drove up the driveway, it began to snow. We both knew immediately that we had found our home.

We had many happy days in Rhode Island. Every day after breakfast and before he began to work, we would take a long walk —sometimes for two or three hours—along the beach or through a park or forging a path through the trees in a local forest. He hated to take the marked paths—always wanted to find his own. He usually walked with a pair of clippers to cut his way through the thorny brush. Then he would get to work. He was never completely satisfied, always trying to say something new and original. Someone once said to him, "Mr. Quinn, I would give anything to have half your talent." His response was, "You wouldn't want the nightmares that go with it."

Work and play were interchangeable for Tony. He played as he worked and worked as he played. Our daughter, Antonia, once asked him, "Papa, why don't you have a job?" He said, "My job is making you proud that I'm your papa."

In marriage, as in his work, he would never accept idleness. He believed we should grow together, learn together—discover poetry, rocks, trees, and birds together—and we did, until the very end.

He would read me his favorite poems, teach me how colors and textures affected a painting, or point out a shell on the beach. Every day was a miracle to Tony. Each accomplishment with the children was a great victory. Teaching them to ride a two-wheel bicycle gave him more pleasure than receiving a lifetime achievement award. And although fear and insecurity were a big part of his character, he felt these were important emotions to have and to conquer in order to succeed in life. "An actor can only be as good as he dares to be bad."

Tony never gave in to his fear. A line from a favorite poet of his youth, Alfred Tennyson, was the motto by which he lived:

To strive, to seek, to find, and not to yield.

Anthony and Katherine, 1998

His Mind, His Eye,

and His Hand

Jay Parini

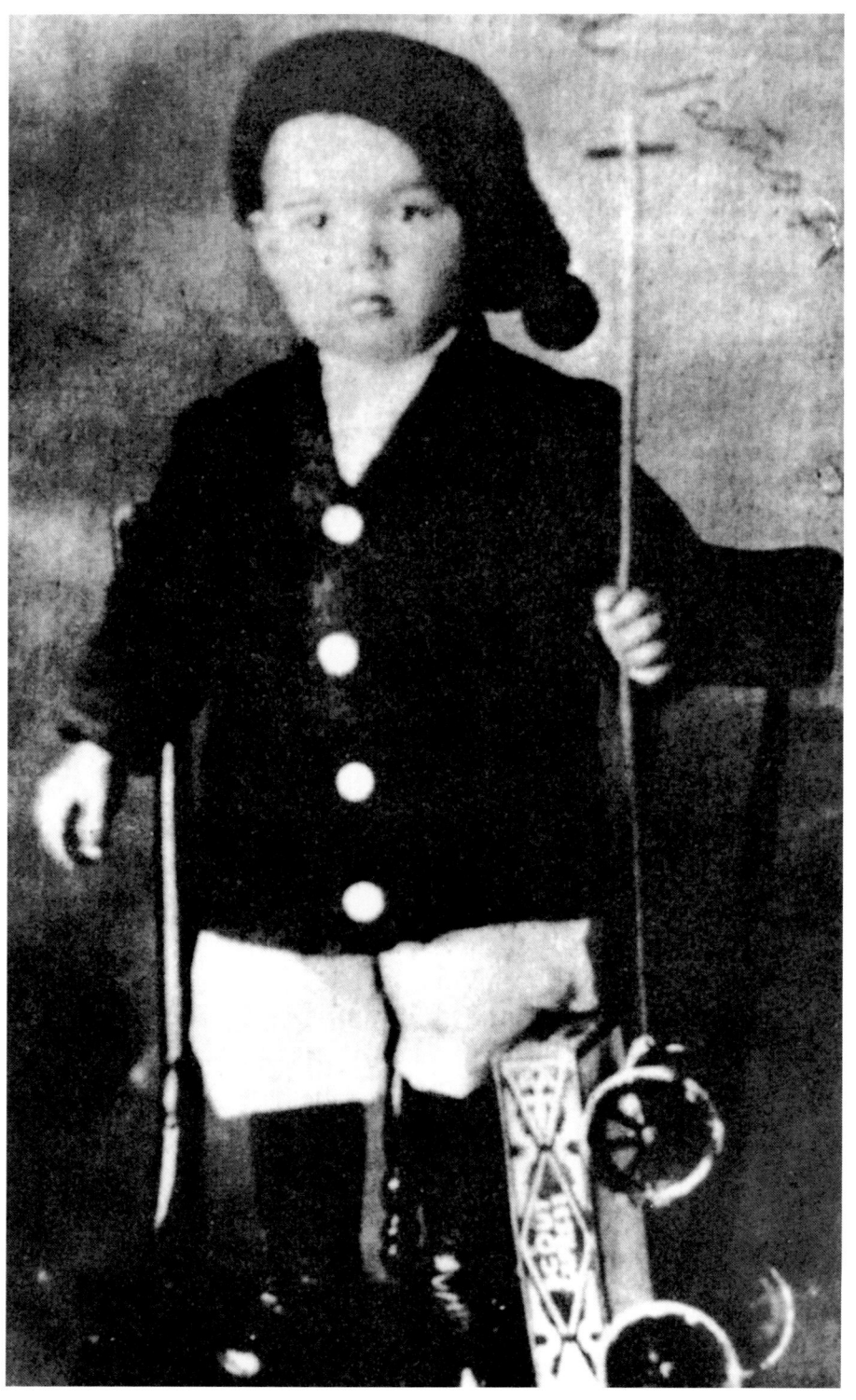

Anthony at eighteen months, 1916

Anthony Quinn's Eye is a sumptuous book that reflects, quite literally, the view of an artist. Leafing through its colorful pages, one encounters the world of one of the most interesting men of our time, an actor and artist who never ceased to create compelling work on whatever canvas he chose. He summoned a vision of reality and declared it pure, in his daily life, his family, and his work. This collection of photographs pays tribute to many aspects of a man who gave so much of himself over six decades—to his family, his friends, his millions of fans.

Born in rural Mexico, in poverty, Quinn lifted himself high, becoming a world-famous, award-winning actor on stage and in film. He is, of course, most widely known for his riveting performances in films like *La Strada, Viva Zapata!, Lust for Life,* and *Zorba the Greek*—just to name a few of the hundreds of major films that established him as one of the preeminent actors of his day. He performed on Broadway in important productions throughout the years, as with his lead role in the original production of *A Streetcar Named Desire,* by Tennessee Williams, and the hugely successful stage version of *Zorba the Greek*. Everyone remembers Quinn in these roles as the earthy, life-loving, exuberant man of the world who survives by his energy, his wits, his unquenchable fire.

In a sense, Quinn was not acting. He was, indeed, a force of nature, a version of the man he played so memorably on screen and stage. I knew him personally, as a friend, and experienced at close range his immense vitality, his thrust of being, his profound wish to create a world around him that matched his inner vision. Art and literature played a significant role in his life, helping him to shape this vision. He read constantly: Tolstoy and Shakespeare were the companions of his later years, their words ringing in his head. He also leafed through his magnificent collection of art books, absorbing the work of the masters: Michelangelo, Leonardo da Vinci, Titian, Vincent van Gogh, Paul Gauguin. He especially loved Cézanne, Matisse, and Picasso—artists who absorbed and translated the peculiar and affecting light of the Mediterranean. One can see, at a glance, in Quinn's work the special attention paid to Picasso, the great Spaniard, with whom he identified. Quinn and Picasso seemed to share a visceral response to the world of light and color, shape and texture.

Tony and I spent hours talking about Picasso, about that artist's love for women and children, about his insistent drive to refashion the world around him, to arrange and rearrange reality. Cubism, which Picasso defined as "a dance around the object," fascinated Tony, who pored over Picasso's paintings and sculptures in museums and books, studying them until they became a part of his own soul. I remember one morning when I

Playing chess on the set of
The Secret of Santa Vittoria, 1969

Studio, Bristol

stood beside him in his studio in New York as he worked on a magnificent piece of sculpture. He said to me, "Picasso understood that reality is not something you can take for granted. He made reality, with his own hands." As he said this, his own large, rough hands worked, fashioning a thing of grace and beauty, molding a piece of art from the amorphous world around him. He was making his world, remaking the world in his own image, in the shimmer of his imagination.

Tony Quinn never stopped making things. From boyhood, he was a visual artist, always doodling, drawing faces, tracing images on the napkin on his table, in the sand beneath his feet. He put things together in odd ways, making collages. He snipped and clipped, glued and hacked, sketched and painted—this activity was part of his being. It was involuntary, a natural process. His eye and mind never lost contact with his hands, which moved quickly and lovingly, embracing the world, taking it apart, studying it, putting it back together in novel ways. This was true to

Everywhere Tony went, he was surrounded by children. He drove Antonia to school every day. He spent every possible minute of the day with our children. That's the way he wanted it. I told him we had to let them have their space, spend time with their friends—he said, "Invite their friends over here, as many as they want." And so it was, the house was always full of children. We'd all have dinner, sometimes home, sometimes out in restaurants. Afterwards the children would put on a show—Tony and I were the audience. For him, it was better than Broadway.

Dancing the *Zorba* dance in his hometown of Chihuahua, Mexico. Left to right: Patricio Martinez (governor of Chihuahua), Anthony, Katherine, Antonia, and Ryan, 2000

Fixing bicycle wheel in Libya

the end of his life, when he settled into the seaside home in Rhode Island pictured in this book, making a final gesture of creativity in a place of serene beauty, with its prospect of the sea, its lush gardens, its spacious rooms full of light and color.

His last years were graced by his marriage to Katherine and the arrival of his last two children, Antonia and Ryan. Tony Quinn relished the role of father and husband and poured himself into the lives of his children. He himself had the mind of a child, which is to say, the mind of an artist. Each day was a day of discovery for him, a day of learning and making. Like a child, he stood open-eyed before the natural world, absorbing its splendor, its pain, its infinite mutations. That childlike stance before the mysteries of existence modified his view of things and played into the texture of the world that he created: the big, airy rooms of his home, filled with paintings and books, African masks,

Bronze cast of hands:
Anthony, Ryan, and Antonia

and tactile objects. This was a dream world come into sudden being, a palpable existence, caught in the pages of this book, which offers a peek into the life that Anthony Quinn shaped and fashioned with his bare hands, his exquisite eye, his omnivorous mind.

Anthony Quinn's Eye is a feast of light and color, a glimpse into a special reality. It contains images of Tony throughout his life, as in an early self-portrait, which I remember vividly. For a couple of years I worked with Tony on a script, sitting opposite him at a long table, looking at a self-portrait that he had painted in his youth, comparing it with the rugged, handsome, mobile face of his old age. It was almost surreal, turning from the painting to the reality, from youth to age, from fiction to fact. I was lucky enough to see the world through his eyes with him beside me. I got a tour of that tactile, playful world, with Tony as a patient guide. This book is the next best thing: it looks at the world of Anthony Quinn with a shrewd intimacy, offering glimpses, long views, a steady gaze. I suspect that few readers will come away from this book unchanged, unmoved.

On a trolley in San Francisco with
Katherine and Ryan, 2000

In high school, Tony's architectural drawings won a prize, which was a meeting with Frank Lloyd Wright. Wright liked his drawings but told him that to be successful he needed to improve his speech. That required an operation on his frenulum, and afterwards, for speech therapy, he started acting classes. He worked as a janitor to pay for the lessons, and on his way home, he would stop by an antique shop to admire this horse. Week after week, he'd stop to contemplate it, until the owner came out and negotiated a deal. Tony could buy the horse, paying ten or twenty cents a week until it was all settled. He had that horse from the time he was seventeen.

T'ang horse, Anthony's first acquisition

Collected pieces

FOLLOWING PAGE Library, Bristol

Anthony at age eighty-five, Bristol

He had an obsession with books, always reading. He educated himself as an artist through his art books. Anywhere we went, the first thing he did was go to a bookstore. This collection of Shakespeare belonged to John Barrymore. They met backstage when Tony was playing a part based on Barrymore. They grew very close, even though Tony was not yet twenty and Barrymore, much older, lived a notoriously dissolute life. When Barrymore was dying, Tony spent long hours at his bedside. After his death, Tony bought this collection from the estate.

Library, Bristol

Breakfast room with collected pieces, Bristol
Tapestry at far end by Anthony, c.1980

Masks from Anthony's collection

He collected eggs, more for their beauty than for their value. The collection was right near the breakfast table, where Tony could admire it every day, but also where it was a temptation for the children. Instead of forbidding them to touch, he made a game out of it. He'd have them pick out just one. And he'd make it seem especially important, pointing out colors and shapes in the design. Then he'd have them bring him another one, and he'd do the same thing. They learned the eggs weren't taboo, and they appreciated them as he did.

Looking through the egg collection into the breakfast room, Bristol

ABOVE AND FOLLOWING PAGES Home in Bristol

Tony was always studying hands, sketching hands, trying to get them just right. We were all with him in a foundry that was casting a bronze sculpture of his. Our daughter, Antonia, was three and getting restless. The owner took her to make a mold of her hand, then cast it in plaster and later in bronze. It was a beautiful little hand.

A couple of years later, when Ryan was three, we were back at the foundry and Tony wanted Ryan's hand done, too. I told Tony to do his own hand as well. He had such wonderful, gnarly hands, weathered by time. He growled and grumbled, but did it. Reluctantly.

Small cast-bronze hands of Anthony, Antonia, and Ryan at left
Triumph, 1987, painting over mantle
Song of Zorba, c.1984, sculpture in foreground

He was doing these little figures to keep himself occupied while he was making Lion of the Desert *in Libya. He set up a wood shop in a trailer. When he had done a few pieces, he was told that local law banned representations of women in art. So he started doing more abstract figures.*

From a train window, while crossing the desert, he saw all these discarded figurative sculptures. Pieces of bodies, worn away by sun and wind and sand. He wanted to achieve that same effect. That's why so many of his pieces have holes, as if parts have been washed away by time.

He saw art in almost everything. He would find things and keep them, never throw them away, because he saw something special in them. We were in a Chinese restaurant with the children, and the wallpaper had these swipes of color. He looked at them and said, "There's a woman's ass up there." I was skeptical. So he pointed out the curve of her back and, damn it, I saw it. He was looking at this terrible wallpaper, and he saw something beautiful in it.

Collected sculpture

Indian swing sculpture, Bristol

Barn studio, Bristol

Painting studio with tapa cloth wall covering made out of New Zealand tree bark, Bristol

He was always beautifying his surroundings with little enhancements. That's what he did in the barn. He'd buy an old bronze or iron piece in an antique or junk shop, and then he'd find just the right home for it on a wall or on a post—it added a special touch, gave everything a personality. Once we were in a hotel in Miami. The walls in the suite were bare. He complained to the manager that he could not stand bare walls. They went to a local gallery and brought back two dozen posters for him to choose from—he chose ten, helped hang them, and made sure they were well placed. He sat down and said, "Now doesn't that look better?"

LEFT AND FOLLOWING PAGE Barn studio, Bristol

PAGES 72–73

This is one of the Austrian pines at Bristol that was stricken by a blight. It was dead, so he called the tree man to cut it down. When they cut it down, it had such a beautiful shape to it, he didn't want them to take it away. He said it would be a beautiful bench one day as it got older and older, and he had it put up on the pedestal.

PAGES 74–75

Just outside Rome, he saw this stone in front of a nursery, about four feet tall, full of holes. "That's a beautiful stone," he said. He told the owner, "I want to take it home and make a sculpture out of it." Although it was not for sale, the owner agreed to let him have it. Walking through the nursery, there were more stones like it. "I want that one…and that one…." Altogether there were eight pieces. He paid a thousand dollars for them all. (It cost nine thousand to ship them home.) It turned out the first stone was half buried. When it was taken out of the ground, it was twice the size. "Better yet!" Tony said.

I used it as his headstone. It is the centerpiece in the garden on our property where he is buried.

PAGES 76–77

Anywhere we traveled, he'd pick things up off the ground—rocks, pieces of wood. He always thought there was some beauty in them he had to find and rescue. By the time we left, we'd have a suitcase full of rocks to bring home. One time we carried home more things we'd collected than clothes we'd brought with us.

In a restaurant in Brazil, they displayed their fish around a piece of driftwood. He said he wanted to buy it. They thought he meant one of the fish. But no, it was the wood he wanted. So we had it on the table during dinner, hauled it back to the hotel, packed it in the suitcase, and brought it home.

African art in barn, Bristol

Anthony, c.1963

Making and Collecting Art:

Anthony Quinn's Search for Intimacy through Creativity

Donald Kuspit

Rehearsing with Alan Bates on the beach in Crete during the filming of *Zorba the Greek*, 1964

Tony was always drawing. In Crete, during the filming of Zorba, he'd have to wait hours for an operator to put through overseas phone calls. He'd sit doing sketch after sketch and throw them all in a drawer. He was sharing a house with his photographer friend, Sam Shaw. One day they were at the flea market, buying artifacts and things for the house, when Sam noticed some sketches for sale. "They look just like yours, Tony." They were his sketches. The housekeeper was stealing them and selling them.

Sketching on the beach in Crete

Anthony Quinn made many paintings, sculptures, and, above all, drawings and sketches, often of faces, sometimes of bodies, at other times abstractions, remotely imagistic, but essentially studies in form. He also collected paintings and sculptures by other artists, particularly Mediterranean modernists. A large blue nude by Matisse held a prominent place in his home. This late work—a climactic abstract statement of the odalisque-arabesque (the nude as ornamental shape, hermetically isolated) that engaged Matisse from the beginning of his career—signals Quinn's abiding interest in the female figure, evident particularly in many of his own sculptures. In addition, Quinn owned many African masks and sculptures, a huge collection of decorative eggs—proudly displayed in all their colorful variety—and rare books. Finally, and perhaps most revelatory, he had a taste for oddly shaped rocks and coral—fragments of nature with a rugged intensity resembling his own.

What was all this collecting about? It provided, undoubtedly, a source of inspiration for Quinn's creativity. His own paintings tend to be modernist in spirit, with many showing a clear debt to Picasso, especially in what might be called his Cubo-surrealist phase. More broadly, Quinn's works show Expressionist energy and distortion. Color is often abrupt, standing out from the image with sensuous autonomy. Did Quinn surround himself with things of idiosyncratic beauty to confirm his own idiosyncratic, versatile identity? He was clearly a connoisseur—every object he collected was unique, meaning that it was irreducibly individual whatever its cultural significance—however much he seemed to collect in quantity. The particularity of

FOLLOWING PAGE Etching, c.1948

an object—its materiality as well as its inventiveness—mattered a great deal to him. Werner Muensterberger, an expert on the psychology of collecting, argues that the avid collector accumulates "good" objects to replace the "bad" objects, or the deprivations, of his childhood. His "family" of objects fills the void his biological family created. Collecting is thus a compensatory and self-creating act. Quinn's personal history seems to support Muensterberger's theory. According to Quinn's autobiography, *The Original Sin: A Self-Portrait* (1972), he grew up in great poverty, and suffered the tragic early death of his father. As though to supply himself with emotional nourishment later in life, he collected art—good art that aesthetically as well as expressively held its own. In this sense, his collection is not a cabinet of curiosities but a statement of values.

It is noteworthy that *La Strada* is the first film mentioned in Quinn's autobiography. He described the lead character as a "poor bastard...who had lived a rough, meaningless life. He had never felt love. When he finally found it, he hadn't known what to do—except destroy it." In the final beach scene, he experiences the "eternity of loneliness," represented by the "immensity of space" that is his fate. For me, Quinn was at his greatest in *La Strada*: he inhabited the role of the tragic strongman who denies his own need for human intimacy and love—represented by his relationship with the clownlike waif, a vulnerable, caring woman—while desperate for them. Quinn showed how the wish for strength and self-sufficiency can lead to folly and self-defeat. In this role, acting and being became one. It is an amazing feat of creativity. On one level, art allowed Quinn to recover that same moment—when creative acting becomes all too human, when acting becomes consummate art. The works he created and collected embodied that precious moment, what Virginia Woolf called "moments of being"—existence at its most essential and pure.

More immediately—and urgently—Quinn made art to be himself rather than to be someone else. I think what he wanted from art—the art of others and his own—was a sanctuary from his public identity as an actor. I think he sought refuge from acting in being. Instead of playing a role, in which he was indirectly himself, he struggled to represent himself as directly as possible. Phyllis Greenacre has suggested that the actor is a kind of imposter, meaning that he wants to be known for the make-believe self he plays rather than for his real self. He can only find himself through theater, yet the self he finds is not really his own. In fact, he doesn't know who he really is, which is why he is unable to be genuinely creative. According to Hanna Segal, this means to be able to create works of art that can stand on their own even as they represent the artist's innermost self. Quinn was tired of posing—of the "as if" position of inauthenticity that acting puts one in, even when it demands that the actor draw on the resources of whatever self he has—and wanted to be truly himself. He was determined to be what Donald Winnicott called a "true creative self" rather than a "false compliant self," which means a visceral, not simply a social, self. And there is a great deal of determination and viscerality in Quinn's works. In short, Quinn was desperate for authenticity, and he

Painting, c. 1951

Painting, 1980

92

Sam Shaw gave him these books. A friend of Sam's would cover simple photo albums with African fabric. Tony would put his little sketches in these books. He liked to keep things organized—black-and-white drawings in one book, color drawings in another, abstracts, sculpture studies, all in their own books. He needed order in his life. "If your life is not in order," he would say, "you cannot create."

PAGES 94–111 Drawings by Anthony, 1950–2001

became authentic by making and collecting art, that is, by identifying with genuine art—art that unequivocally expresses the genuine self.

The paradox of such an art is that it embodies the creative apperception—to use Winnicott's term—of the other. It is possible only through intimacy—what might be called creative intimacy. A further paradox: such intimacy opens the way to intuition of the elemental in life and brings with it the capacity to represent the elemental creatively.

The erotic motif is a constant in Quinn's works. Again and again he struggles to quintessentialize it. The female form is its essence, and he essentializes the female form until it becomes pure eros. It is an aesthetic process of idealization, refining the form toward pure abstraction—which means that it becomes less and less intimate. However, Quinn rebounds to intimacy in his portrait sketches. To me they are his most expressively intriguing as well as stylistically varied work. Face after face appears, like memories from the past, captured in all their transience, yet durable. Some of the works are of women, but shown now as individuals—with faces, not simply bodies, even when they have bodies, as in a 1975 drawing—rather than erotic objects. Quinn mastered the face and, above all, the range of its expressions, often showing introspective, pensive human beings, usually with a touch of melancholy, less often showing them smiling, as though engaging other human beings. There are full faces, three-quarter faces, and profiles, all filled with expressive life. Sometimes they veer sharply toward pure form, such as a 1976 drawing that looks like a grand abstract gesture, in which the face is subsumed in swirling lines; at other

times they seem satiric, or at least ironical, especially when certain details are emphasized, such as the monocle in a 1975 drawing. Many of the drawings are sensitive line studies. The lines are few and deft, leaving most of the paper untouched, transforming it into pure space—always the sign of a successful drawing. The faces are living portraits in the deepest sense: they convey inward life through external form. Physiology becomes expressive physiognomy, which is the goal of portraiture. The human face is endlessly fascinating, the site of individuality, and Quinn conveys the fascination of idiosyncratic individuals, with no loss of descriptive precision.

The African masks and sculptures that Quinn collected and, especially, the coral and stones that he treasured—in effect, found expressionistic sculpture—are much more explicitly elemental than the portraits. The latter, after all, are social as well as personal—the two are inextricable in a good portrait—while the primitive and natural artifacts are neither: they are transparently primordial. Still, this same raw primordiality appears in a 1975 expressionistic painting of a demonic figure and in the Fauvist colors of a portrait sketch of a woman. They convey the energy that Quinn brought to his strongman role in *La Strada*—the same proud strength, tempered by unexpected vulnerability. The painting is dark, yet the figure is set in acid yellow; the Fauvist colors of the portrait are contradicted by its strong black outline. The mixture of the elemental and the melancholy is also evident in an early self-portrait.

Taken as a whole, Quinn's collection and oeuvre—and his collection is implicitly part of his oeuvre—show a distinctive mix of modernist primitivism and formalism. They are emotionally and

Study for sculpture "Zeus"

formally primitivist, in Robert Goldwater's sense of those terms: they articulate human irrationality through artistic means that seem irrational and alien by traditional Western standards, even as they aesthetically rationalize them. They are intimate works created and collected by a person who was able to use art to explore and express himself and to capture the qualities of others, demonstrating that art remains bound to the human condition. Quinn was always sketching, and his sketches seem his most aesthetically and expressively realized works, suggesting that spontaneity was more important to him than finish, as it is for many modern masters, and indicating that self-realization through art—through his own free hand rather than through the artifice of a scripted role—was a constant need necessary for his psychic survival.

106

He was shaving in the bathroom of a hotel outside Las Vegas. He liked the view from the window so much, he stood in the bathroom and sketched it. I wondered why he was taking so long, and there he was, sketching.

Sketching with Antonia, Katherine, and Ryan, c.1997

Before Antonia was a year old, he'd put a pencil in her hand and she'd push it around and make a scribble. Tony would look at it and say, "That's a beautiful drawing." And he would outline part of the scribble and find a form in it, a bird or a face. She made this collage of colored paper and he drew around it, bringing out the shape of a mask. He signed these works A·A Quinn because he didn't want to take the credit for himself. She loved that.

When Ryan was three, he made a scribble, and Tony said, "That's a wonderful drawing of a dancing man." When he outlined the dancing figure, Ryan started screaming, "Papa, you ruined my drawing. It wasn't a man, it was a race car." And Tony told him, "You're right. That's your drawing, not mine." And he never drew over their drawings again.

Sketch done with Antonia, signed accordingly, 1994

Sketch/collage done with Antonia, 1994

Sketch done with Ryan, c.1998

Tony's first son, Christopher, drowned when he was three in a neighbor's fish pond. The neighbor was W. C. Fields. Tony always had a fear of our children drowning. When we first bought the house in Bristol, there was a beautiful indoor pool. He kept it for six months or so, but he couldn't sleep, worrying about the children. He had it boarded over and turned it into his painting studio.

Painting studio, Bristol

FOLLOWING PAGE Working on self-portrait, 2000

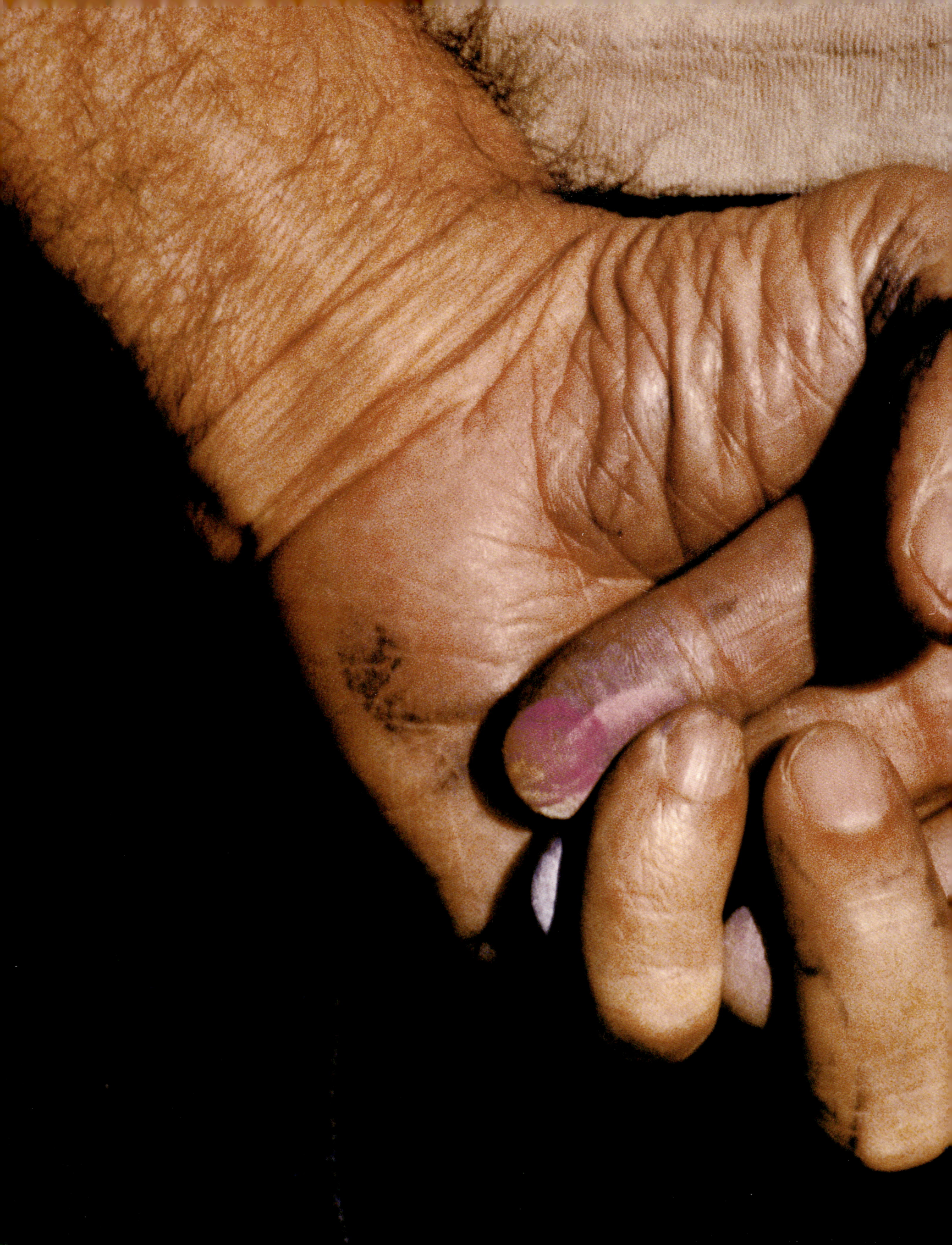

120

Self-portrait as Pope Kyril in *The Shoes of the Fisherman*, c.1993

Working on self-portrait, 1982
Photograph taken and signed by
his friend Sam Shaw

When Tony was a child in El Paso, the view from the window was of the trash outside.

His father painted a mountain scene on the window so they wouldn't have to look at the trash.

This was a studio of his that didn't have much of a view. So he put wooden panels in the windows and painted a better view, just like his father.

Painting in Rome

Self-portrait, 1932

Ibo Dance, c.1982

Of Age, 2000

Escort for Hire, c.2000

He would show me something, some food or a piece of cloth, and ask me to find him that color. I had no art experience, but I would help him mix colors. Then I made this card to show him what each color looked like once it was painted on a surface and dried. And I printed the name of the color next to each one. He liked that kind of order. Fat brushes in one container, skinny brushes in another, oils in one, acrylics in another. Very organized.

Paintings in progress, Bristol, 2001

FOLLOWING PAGE Working on *Triumph*, 1987

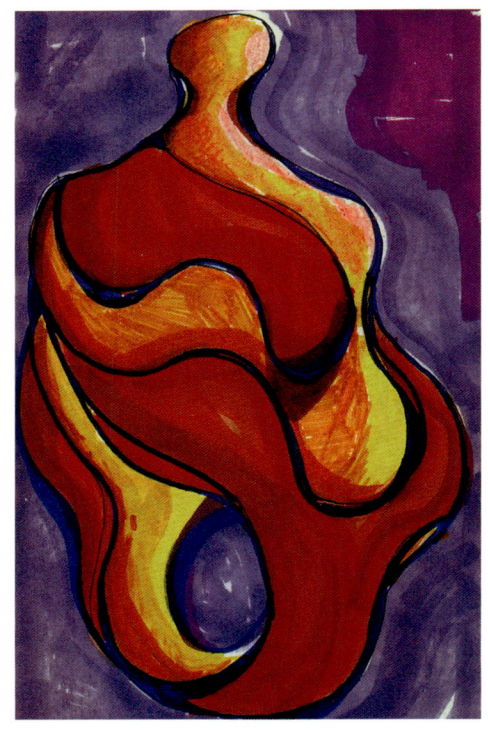

Anthony R. Quinn

PAGES 134–143 Sketches and studies for sculptures and paintings, 1980–2001

PRECEDING PAGE An unfinished work about the Mexican Revolution, from the series *Unfulfilled Promises*

137

LEFT Drawing done with Antonia, 1994

RIGHT Drawing done with Antonia, 1994

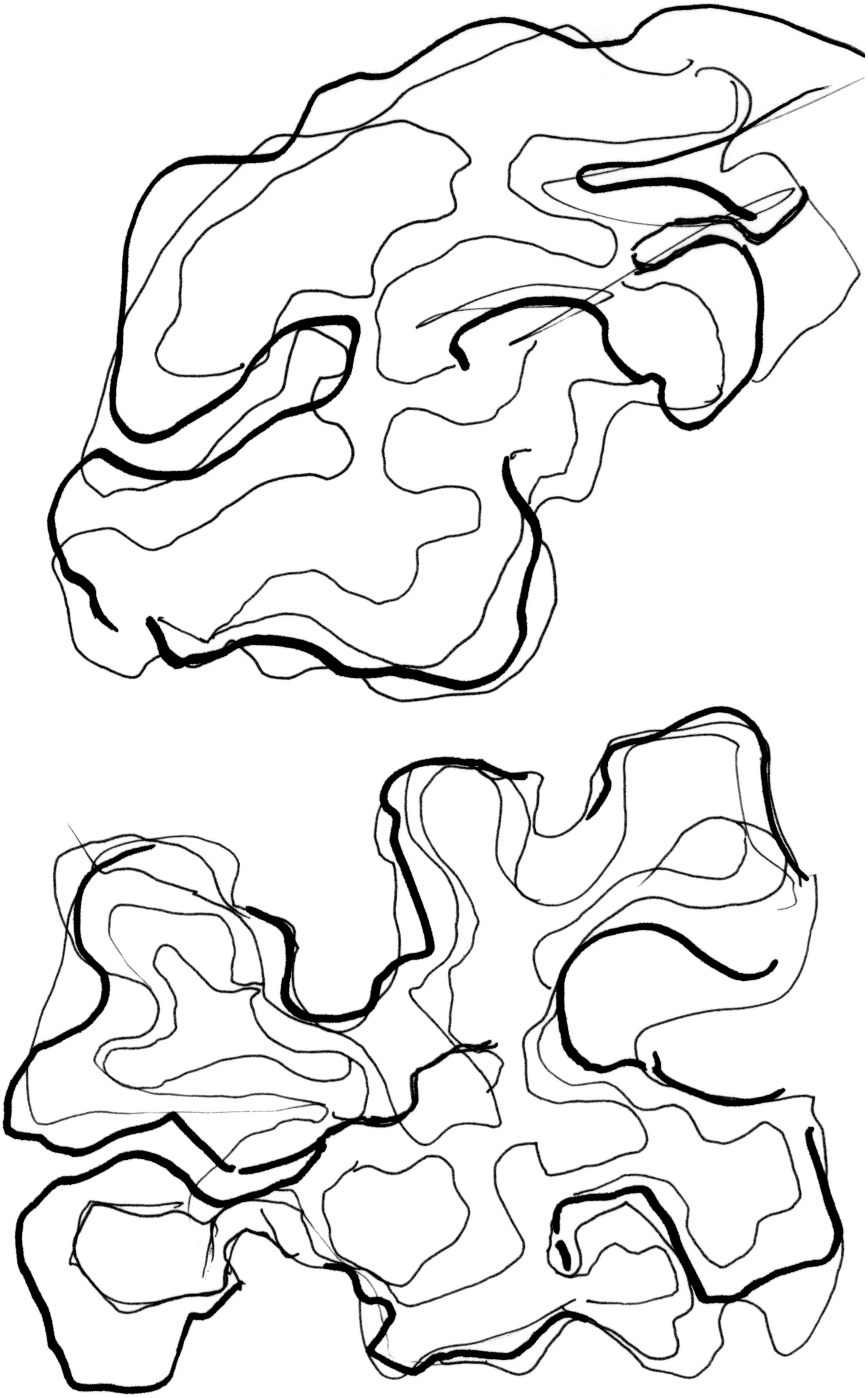

144 THIS PAGE AND FOLLOWING PAGES *The Great Spirit,* 1985. Collection of 20 stone lithographs and sculpture inspired by the poetry and wisdom of the native people of North America

RITES AND CEREMONIES

The torturing scene (or pohk-hong as they called it) commenced within, in the following manner.

The young men reclining around the sides of the Medicine Lodge, who had now reached the middle of the fourth day without eating, drinking, or sleeping, and consequently weakened and emaciated, commenced to submit to the operation of the knife and other instruments of torture.

Two men, who were to inflict the tortures, had taken their positions near the middle of the lodge; one, with a large knife with a sharp point and two edges, which were hacked with another knife in order to produce as much pain as possible, was ready to make the incisions through the flesh,

39

or a groan; but when the turning commenced, they began crying in the most heartrending tones to the Great Spirit; imploring him to enable them to bear and survive the painful ordeal they were entering on. This piteous prayer, the sounds of which no imagination can ever reach, and of which I could get no translation, seemed to be an established form ejaculated alike by all, and continued until fainting commenced, when it gradually ceased.

In each instance they were turned until they fainted and their cries were ended. Their heads hanging forwards and down, and their tongues distended, and becoming entirely motionless and silent, they had, in each instance, the appearance of a corpse. In this view, which was sketched whilst the two young men were hanging before me, one is suspended by the muscles of the breast, and the other by the muscles of the shoulders, and two of the young candidates are seen reclining on the ground, and waiting for their turn.

When brought to this condition, without signs of animation, the lookers-on pronounced the word *dead! dead!* when the men who had turned them struck the cords with their poles, which was the signal for the men on top of the lodge to lower them to the ground, — the time of their suspension having been from fifteen to twenty minutes.

The excessive pain produced by the turning, which

44

The four inside markings on the Wheel represent the Four-Old-Men who are frequently addressed during the ceremony, and who stand watching and guarding the inhabitants of this world. The Four-Old-Men may also be called the gods of the four world quarters, and to them the Sun Dance priest often makes supplication that they may live to a great age (...) They therefore represent the living element of all people. If the wind blows from the north, it is said to come from the Old-Man-of-the-North, who controls the wind of that end or quarter of the world. Another priest states more definitely that the Four-Old-Men are Summer, Winter, Day and Night, who though they travel in single file, yet are considered as occupying the four cardinal points. Thus, according to direction and the Arapaho color scheme, Day and Summer are the Southeast and Southwest, respectively, and are black in color, while Winter and Night are the Northwest and Northeast, respectively, and are red in color. Inasmuch as Sun is regarded as the Grandfather of the Four-Old-Men, it is more than likely that the Wheel may be regarded as the emblem of the Sun.

George A. DORSEY, 1903.

partly to rise, and move their bodies to another part of the lodge, where there sat a man with a hatchet in is hand and a dried buffalo skull before him, his body red, his hands and feet, black, and wearing a mask, they held up the little finger of the left hand towards the Great Spirit (offering it as a sacrifice, as they thanked him audibly, for having listened to their prayers and protected their lives in what they had just gone through), and laid it on the buffalo skull, where the man with the mask, struck it off at a blow with the hatchet, close to the hand.

During the whole time of this cruel part of the ceremonies, the chiefs and other dignitaries of the tribe were looking on, to decide who amongst the young men were the hardiest and stoutest-hearted, who could hang the longest by his torn flesh without fainting, and who was soonest up after he had fainted, — that they might decide whom to appoint to lead a war party, or to place at the most important posts, in time of war.

G. CATLIN. *The Initiation of young men.*

What might I have accomplished if I had been true to the Spirits' wish?

A seed, blown by the wind, lands in a crevice of a bald mountain. Against all odds, it grows. That is its Karma, the choice of the Great Spirit.

The Spirit plants him in difficult, unpleasant, or Nirvana-like surroundings.

Unlike plants, however, man has the gift of movement. He is able to leave his surroundings in search of different fields, defying the wishes of the Spirit.

Man is no different.

I was born in Chihuahua, Mexico under the gunfire of the revolution. The country was in chaos.

My mother took me to North America in search of greener fields. We found a small barren patch. There we settled in our new home, our new land. We learned to live by its particular values of happiness and success. Two absolute necessities of the new culture.

Through hard work and perseverance I found acceptable substitutes — but not contentment.

I wandered across the ocean in search of something to feed the emptiness. I found new friends, new faces, a new wife, new children and still the same anxieties.

Were the spirits angry that I had left the battle scarred hills of Chihuahua?

I tried to shrug it off. I had found new spiritual substitutes. They were less demanding. But the question remained.

I ask myself the question walking across a desert, a lonely beach, but more often among the stone canyons of New York.

The Spirit is silent.

Only a misty vision remains.

I long to feel whole.

Spirit — speak!

I am ready to listen!

Anthony Quinn

Modern Girl, 1993

Stagecraft, 1993

Phoenician Aristocrat, 1993

Caribbean Island, 1990

Circus, 1990

Ouvea, 2000

Wooden Bird, 1981

Painted wood sculptures

Mobile Bird, 1981

Painting palettes and triangle hanging on the wall in Anthony's studio, Bristol

RIGHT AND FOLLOWING PAGE Barn, Bristol

Aphrodite, travertine, c.1984

162

Guinevere, marble, c.1981

PRECEDING PAGE Unpolished stone sculpture, detail

Working on patina of *Zulu Nude*, Bristol, c.1988

Windblown Lady, marble, c.1982

TOP *Soldadera*, marble, c.1986
BOTTOM *Dawn to Dusk*, marble, c.1984

FOLLOWING PAGE Working at a foundry in France, 1995

Tony loved tools, and his tools were organized like his brushes and his paints. Chisels together, saws together, even the Dremel tool that had all these little bits to sand, file, and cut. He had all the bits in their little compartments, very nicely arranged.

Working on a sculpture in Greece, 1963

FOLLOWING PAGE Working on a sculpture in Italy, c. 1977

Working in his hotel room, Washington, DC, 1985

Working on a sculpture in Libya, 1978

In Spain, Tony saw some men about to burn this big pile of wood. He found out they were old oxen yokes, and he thought they were beautiful. He tried to buy them, but the men insisted on giving them to him. He took them home to his studio, added pieces of wood, sculpted them, and cast them in bronze.

His Majesty, front and back, created from oxen yokes and cast in bronze, c. 1990

Contemplation, marble, c.1981

Tony would make sculptures from his little sketches. He'd start with a sketch, cut it out in wood, then cast it in wax or clay or bronze. You can see the stages of development in his work from sketch to cut-out to wood or metal sculpture.

Carving on a wood burl at a foundry in Rhode Island, 1999

Zephyr, marble, c.1992

RIGHT Studies for sculpture

PAGES 184–185

Instead of ugly metal bookends, Tony wanted something interesting to hold up the books, to decorate the bookshelves. So he sculpted his own and cast them in bronze. Each one is different. His gallerist told him if he could make them all the same, they could sell hundreds of them. He wouldn't do them the same, he wanted each to be unique.

PAGES 186–193 Working, 1970–1980

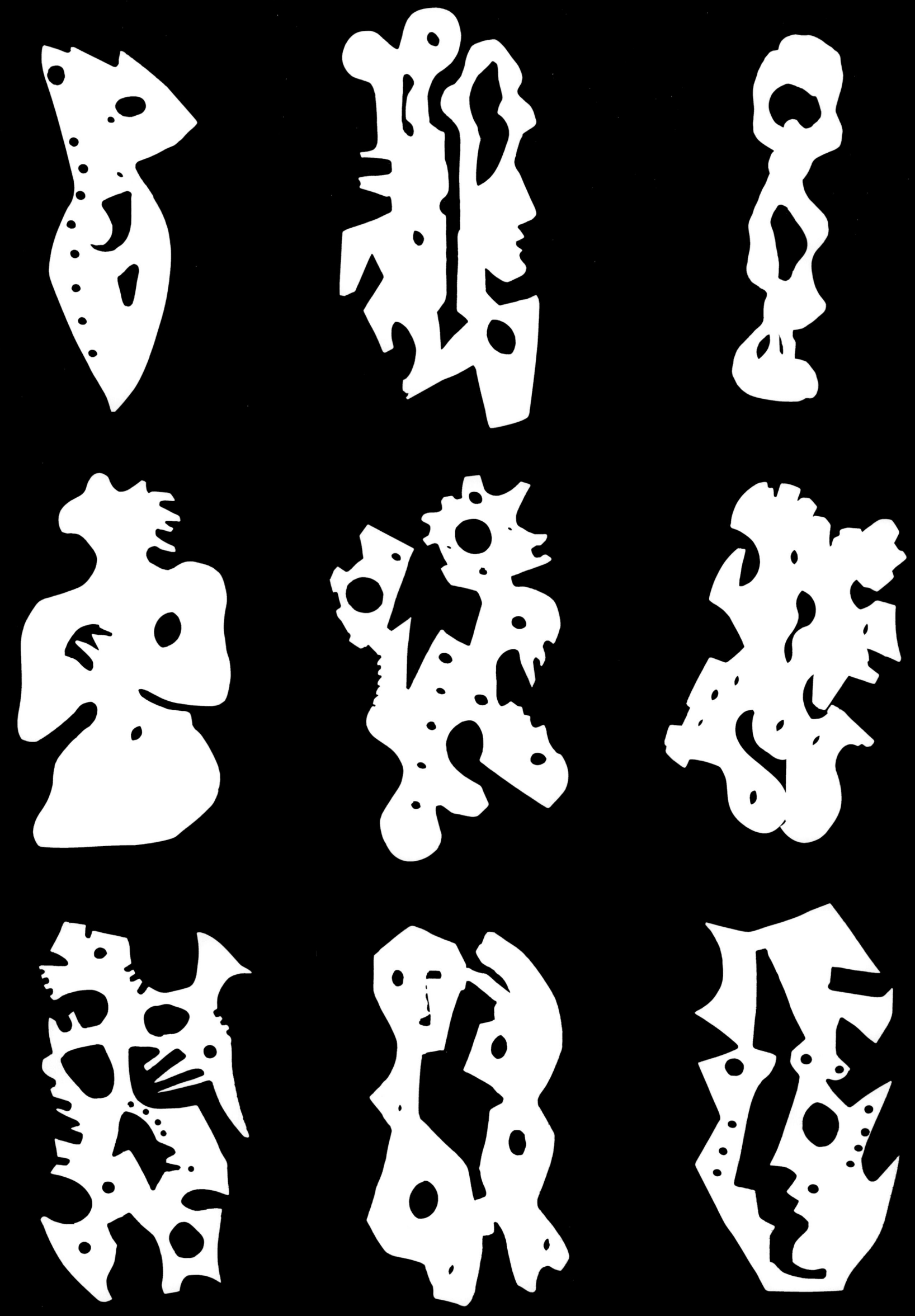

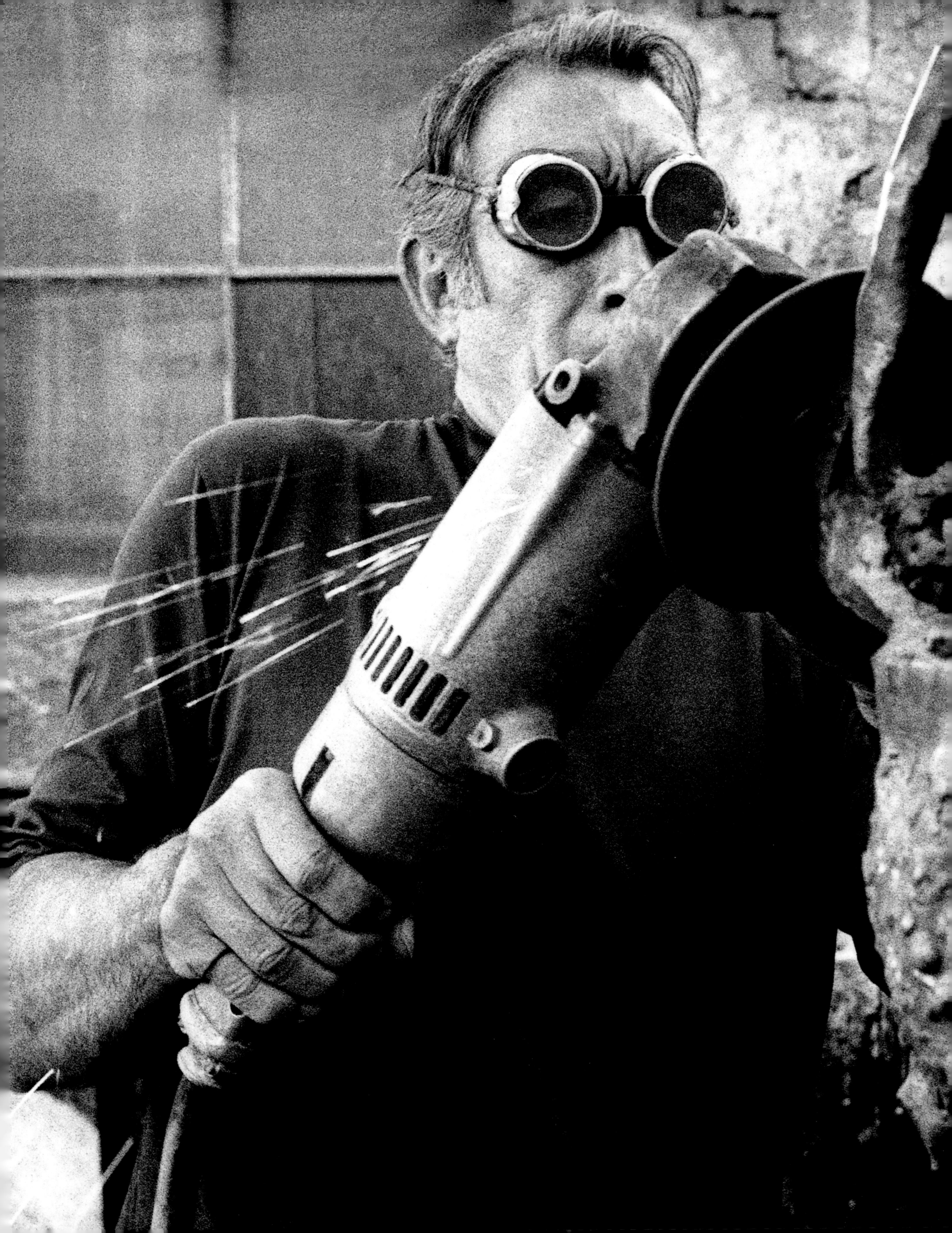

Iron sculptures by Anthony, 1970s

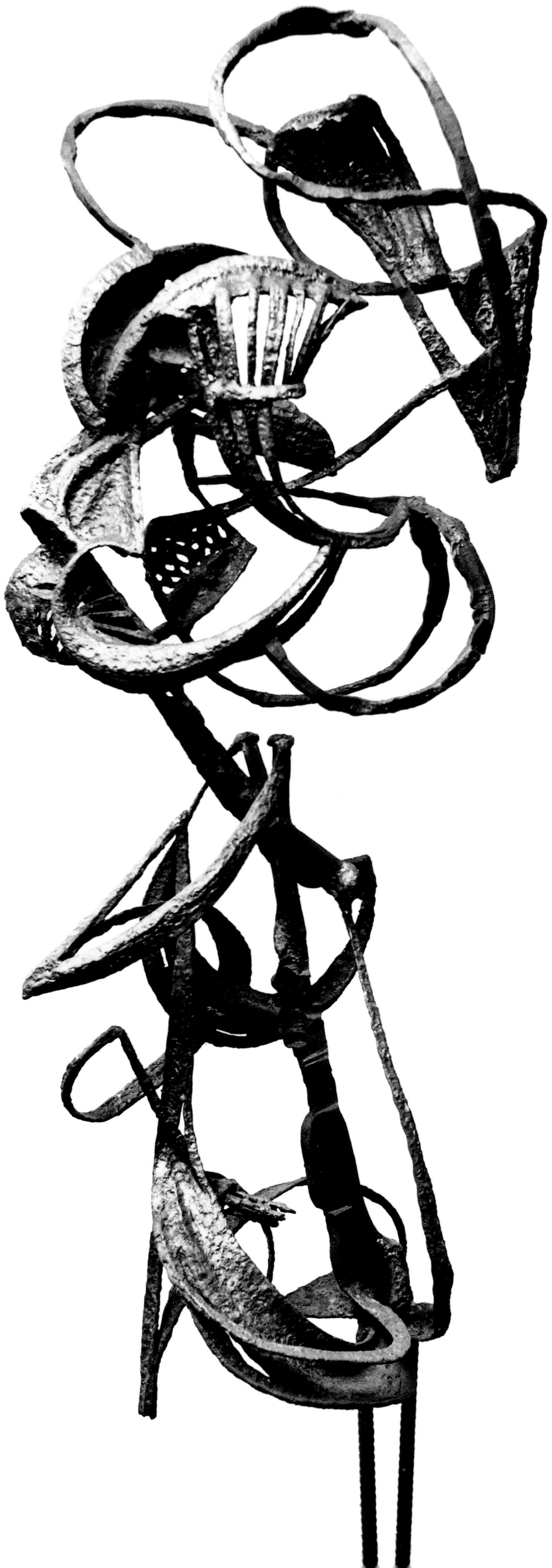

195

196

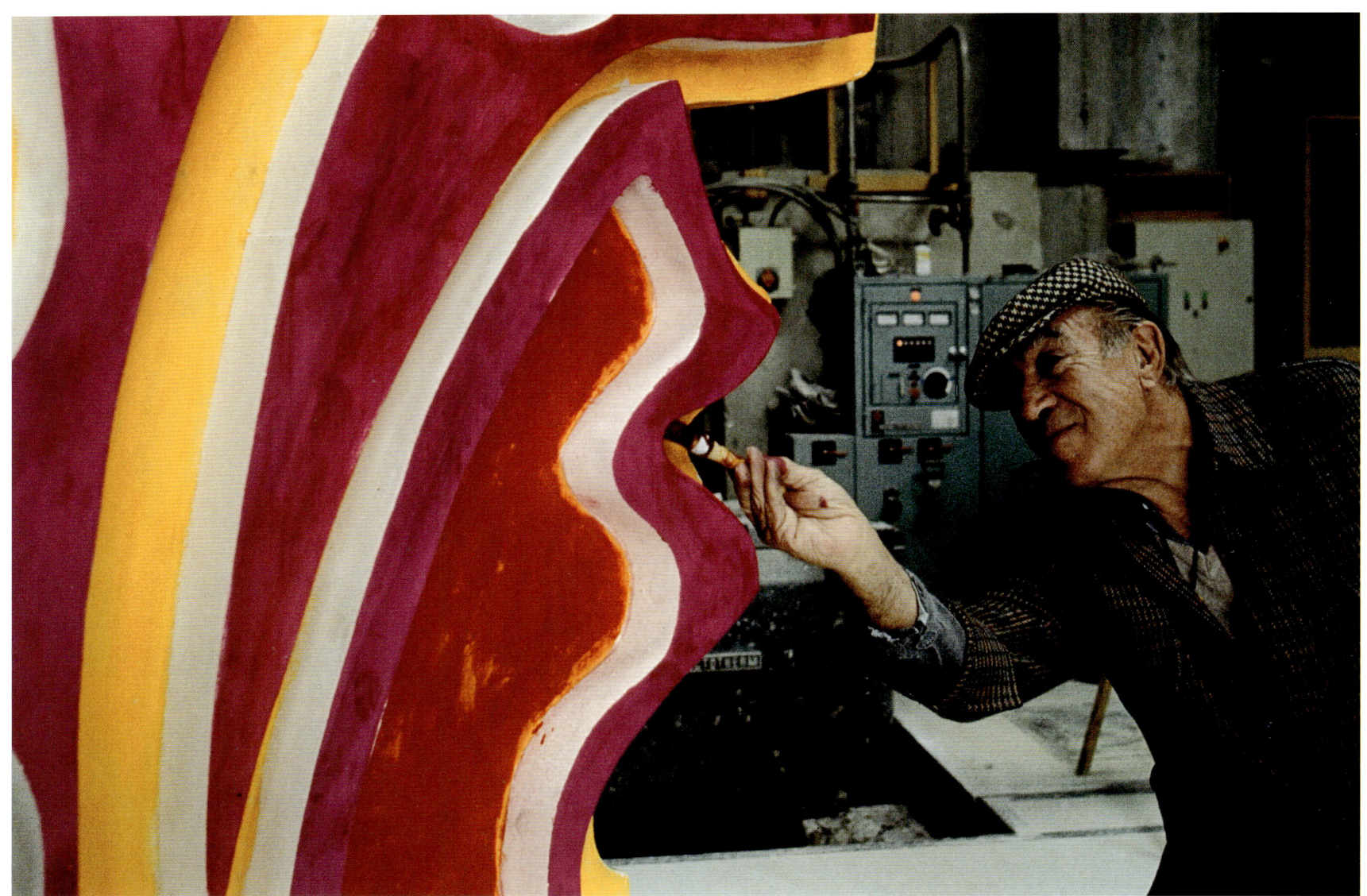

Working in France, c.1991

Bird Yearning to Fly, sketch and wood sculpture, c.1991

Aztec Ancestor, wood, c.1991

FOLLOWING PAGE Sculpture by Anthony gathering "nature's patina" outside barn, Bristol

Scheherezade, travertine, c.1985

206

Innocence, bronze, c.1985

PRECEDING PAGE Marble sculpture by Anthony in barn, Bristol

At a foundry in New York, c.1988

210

PRECEDING PAGE At foundry with daughter Antonia, working on *Diva*, c.1996

At studio in France, c.1991

KIRK DOUGLAS

I have known Tony for so long, it must be at least 50 years. That's a long time to know someone. My respect and admiration for Anthony Quinn have only grown larger through those years. He was a wonderful guy.

It was always a pleasure to be in his company. He was so amusing, so witty, and always a friend.

I have done two films with Tony, 'Last Train from Gun Hill', and 'Lust for Life'. Of course both of these pictures were entirely different. Tony won an Oscar for his portrayal of Gauguin in 'Lust for Life' – deservedly so. He was always a delight to work with.

Tony himself was quite an artist; I admired his talent as a sculptor and as a painter, a talent that was recognized by the world. To me Anthony Quinn is like a fine wine that has passed the test of time. I think of him often and miss him a lot.

Kirk Douglas

A tribute by Kirk Douglas, July 2003

They worked together, and they were lifelong friends and friendly rivals. When they were young and successful, there was only a handful of strong leading actors.

As the years went on, they were even better friends. The last time they spent together was at Kirk's house, not long before Tony died. After dinner, Kirk and Tony were on the floor with Ryan, playing with his pull-back cars. I think they realized how valuable their friendship had been all those years.

On the set of *Lust for Life* with Kirk Douglas, 1956

And now, My Darling, a Kiss —

*[Res**A**pectable] Kiss*

All his scripts are covered with sketches, doodles, writing. He took apart his lines, even the words, wrote them over and over, worked with the words to get the right meaning. He sometimes had trouble memorizing, so he had to use cue cards. Even then, he'd write them out himself. And still he worked over his lines, drew next to them, took them apart, and put them back together. Words were very powerful for him. He would show me how the meaning of a sentence changed depending upon which word the emphasis was placed. He played with the words until they said what he wanted to say.

Acting   Tom Roberts

Few actors can lay claim to the length and breadth of Anthony Quinn's body of work. Across a remarkable sixty-five-year career, he worked with actors from Harold Lloyd to Keanu Reeves, from Laurence Olivier and Katharine Hepburn to Arnold Schwarzenegger and Ann-Margret, and with directors from Cecil B. DeMille to Federico Fellini to Spike Lee.

Launching that career in 1936, Quinn worked within the legendary limitations of the Hollywood system. He was a contract player, performing in whatever picture the studio assigned. That provided some choice opportunities—two Hope and Crosby *Road* pictures, the bullfighting bravura of *Blood and Sand*, and the disturbing lynch-mob parable, *The Ox-Bow Incident*. From his first real role at twenty-one in DeMille's *The Plainsman*, Quinn conveyed the natural poise of an actor with more years and more roles under his belt. That poise never left, even as the sleek beauty of his twenties weathered into what *The New York Times* would later call his "lordly, grizzled charisma."

He was, paradoxically, constrained by his looks and his bearing. His suave Latino handsomeness and his easy masculine manner were not the stuff of 1930s leading men. Ten years earlier, he might have inherited the mantle of Valentino. But the moment of the Latin lover had waned, and his dark, forceful presence consigned Quinn to the supporting roles then classified as "exotics"—ethnic characters, usually villains. He played not only Mexicans—his own heritage—but an endless gallery of Native Americans, Spaniards,

Notebook with script from the stage musical version of *Zorba the Greek*

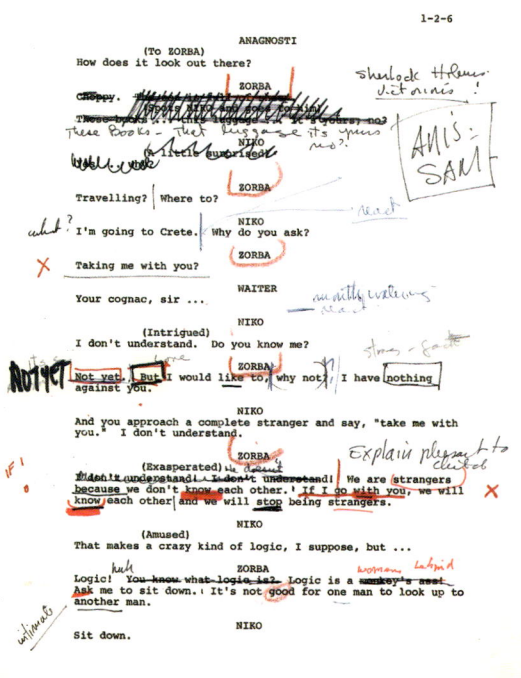
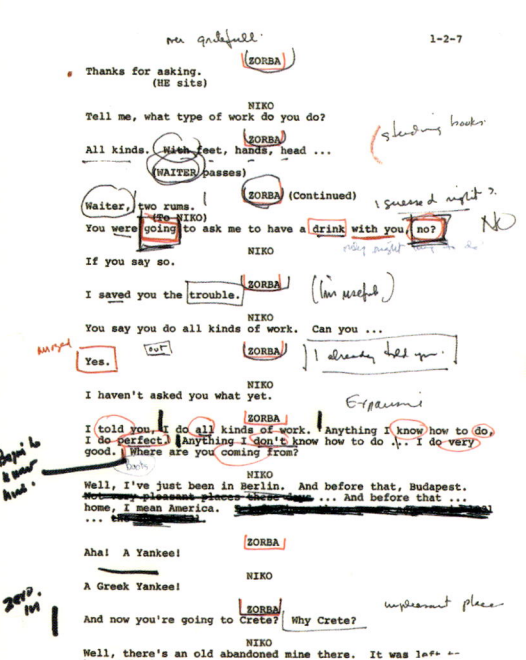
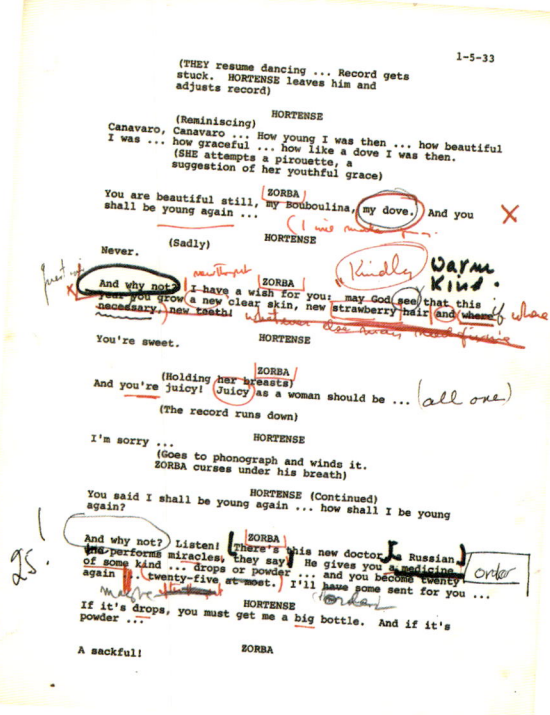

Let me give you the most respectable kiss you've ever had.

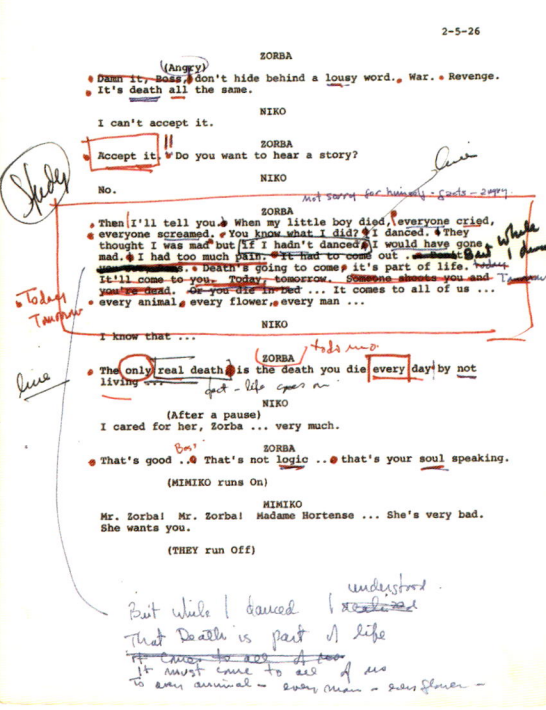

Go to the widow - Boss
Talk to her straight
WITHOUT THINKING
What you are saying to yourself
now
Say to her.

Future. Future is 2 pigs behind
Now is what counts
Now is when you are living

Then like I SAID
Good by
and no looking back

Woman
is like a Fresh Spring
and man is only a Passerby.

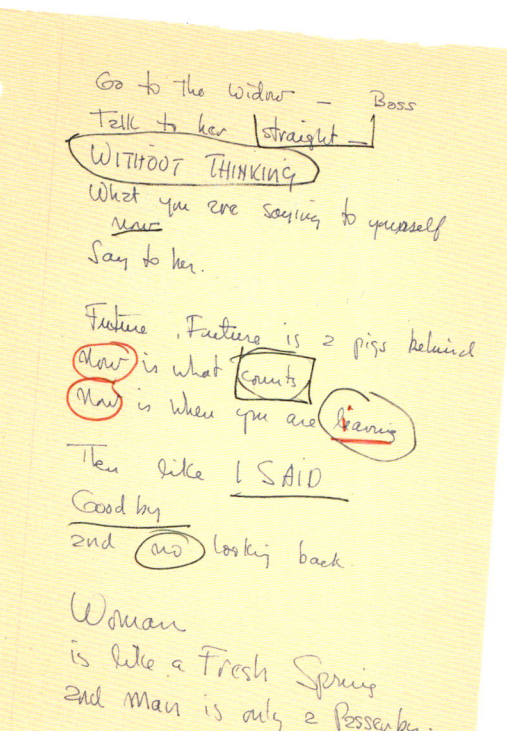

fight
grab to him
Mavrolakis

Cubans, Chinese, Filipinos, Frenchmen, Arabs, Hawaiians, Greeks, and more gangsters and spies than an FBI agent sees in a lifetime.

Even in the stereotyped film universe of virtuous cowboys and barbarous Indians, Quinn brought a dignity, candor, and depth to his Native American characters that have made most of them wear better than many of the cowboy counterparts who vanquished them. No flaring nostrils, no noble poses: Quinn brought an emotional honesty to his exotics that made them, if not less stereotypical, more authentic. Complex though they may have been, these characters were nonetheless cast in adversarial postures to many of the leading players of the day: menacing Gary Cooper in *The Plainsman*; threatening Edward G. Robinson in *Larceny, Inc.*; cracking a whip at Dorothy Lamour in *Road to Singapore*.

By the end of World War II, though, Quinn had grown frustrated with Hollywood's inability to see beyond his ethnic outer layer. After a decade in films, few professional paths lay open that he had not already trod into dust. He could have gone on attacking Erroll Flynn, frightening Bob Hope, and challenging Tyrone Power, but he chose a far more adventuresome course. He headed east.

Many of today's most gifted movie stars occasionally reaffirm their artistry by taking highly publicized turns on the Broadway stage. Quinn beat them to it by fifty years. In 1947, feeling trapped in the slot assigned him by studio chiefs, he abandoned Hollywood for four years of intense stage work and acting study. At a time when Marlon Brando and Montgomery Clift were moving west, Quinn moved his family east and embarked on an educational regimen with the Actors' Studio. Working there with Elia Kazan,

Anthony directing *The Buccaneer* from atop ladder, with Cecil B. DeMille watching from directly below, left, 1958

Quinn succeeded Brando as Stanley in *A Streetcar Named Desire*, playing on Broadway and touring the country for a year. It was extraordinary training for Quinn, who had been a movie actor exclusively for eleven years. It also earned him the respect of Kazan, who four years later would cast him in *Viva Zapata!*, revitalizing Quinn's film career and bringing him his first Academy Award.

It is a measure of his seriousness as an actor that, even after his star shone more brightly on the screen, he still returned periodically to the rigors of the Broadway stage. His 1960 stint as King Henry II opposite Olivier in *Becket* earned Quinn a Tony nomination. In 1983, he returned to Broadway in a musical version of *Zorba the Greek*, playing a character with whom he had become inescapably linked.

But it was the blazing trail he left on the movie screen from 1952 virtually until his death in 2001 that made Anthony Quinn such a presence in the cultural firmament. These are the roles we associate with him, embodying him as a primal force with an unquenchable passion for living. His major gift as an actor was his ability to convey that life force on celluloid, to imprint his three-dimensional personality onto the two-dimensional screen.

Curiously, for all his legendary prowess as a ladies' man, Quinn's onscreen relations with women were mostly troubled. The tragic union of Zampano and Gelsomina in Fellini's *La Strada* is emblematic of the friction that Quinn's characters experienced with women. Tangling with volcanic wife Anna Magnani in *Wild Is the Wind*, with free-spirited daughter Shirley MacLaine in *Hot Spell*, or with temptress Lana Turner in *Portrait in Black* allowed him to portray more complex, self-doubting characters. The steamy dance with Rita Hayworth in *Blood and Sand* or the misty, middle-aged *Walk in the Spring Rain* with Ingrid Bergman are notable exceptions. And his two outings with Sophia Loren, *Black Orchid* and *Heller in Pink Tights*, gave him his most unqualified shots at out-and-out romantic leads.

His most trenchant screen relationships, though, were undoubtedly with men. His two Oscar-winning performances provided dynamic, assured counterpoints to two of Hollywood's strongest actors at their most intense: Marlon Brando in *Viva Zapata!* and Kirk Douglas in *Lust for Life*. Many of Quinn's most enduring films find him inhabiting an almost exclusively male world: *Lawrence of Arabia*, *The Guns of Navarone*, *The Ox-Bow Incident*. Only his signature performance in *Zorba the Greek* finds him balancing equally intimate relationships with both the pathetic Madame Hortense of Lila Kedrova and the introverted Basil of Alan Bates.

His offscreen life, never very private, seemed at times to merge with his onscreen roles, none more so than that of Zorba. The actor and the character became inextricably intertwined in the public eye ever after. He was in some ways confined by that success. Zorba was larger than life, and Quinn infused him with the ideal degree of extravagance, balancing the performance deftly with the others in the film. The public wanted more big performances from him, but Quinn wanted to continue what he had fought to attain, the freedom to choose every sort of role, modest or outrageous, that allowed him to explore new territory. He was not always able to accomplish that, but he left a gallery of indelible screen performances that have permanently secured Anthony Quinn's place in the pantheon of great film actors.

Film, Television, and Theatre

1936 **The Milky Way**
1936 **Parole**
1936 **Sworn Enemy**
1936 **Night Waitress**
1936 **The Plainsman**
1936 **Clean Beds** (theatre)
1937 **Under Strange Flags**
1937 **Swing High, Swing Low**
1937 **Waikiki Wedding**
1937 **The Last Train from Madrid**
1937 **Daughter of Shanghai**
1937 **Partners in Crime**
1938 **The Buccaneer**
1938 **Dangerous to Know**
1938 **Tip-Off Girls**
1938 **Hunted Men**
1938 **Bulldog Drummond in Africa**
1938 **King of Alcatraz**
1939 **King of Chinatown**
1939 **Union Pacific**
1939 **Island of Lost Men**
1939 **Television Spy**
1940 **Emergency Squad**
1940 **Road to Singapore**
1940 **Parole Fixer**
1940 **The Ghost Breakers**
1940 **City for Conquest**
1940 **Texas Rangers Ride Again**
1941 **Blood and Sand**
1941 **Knockout**
1941 **Thieves Fall Out**
1941 **Bullets for O'Hara**
1941 **The Perfect Snob**
1942 **They Died with Their Boots On**
1942 **Larceny, Inc.**
1942 **Road to Morocco**
1942 **The Black Swan**
1943 **The Ox-Bow Incident**
1943 **Guadalcanal Diary**
1944 **Buffalo Bill**
1944 **Roger Touhy, Gangster**
1944 **Ladies of Washington**
1944 **Irish Eyes Are Smiling**
1945 **Where Do We Go from Here?**
1945 **China Sky**
1945 **Back to Bataan**
1946 **California**
1947 **Sinbad the Sailor**
1947 **The Imperfect Lady**
1947 **Black Gold**
1947 **Tycoon**
1947 **The Gentleman from Athens** (theatre)
1948–50 **A Streetcar Named Desire** (theatre)
1949 **Pride's Castle** (television)
1950 **Borned in Texas** (theatre)
1951 **Ned McCobb's Daughter** (television)
1951 **Partners** (television)
1951 **House of Dust** (television)
1951 **Ticket to Oblivion** (television)
1951 **Blue Murder** (television)
1951 **Dark Fleece** (television)
1951 **The Brave Bulls**
1951 **Mask of the Avenger**
1951 **Let Me Hear the Melody** (theatre)
1952 **Viva Zapata!** (Academy Award)
1952 **The Brigand**
1952 **The World in His Arms**
1952 **Against All Flags**
1953 **City Beneath the Sea**
1953 **Seminole**
1953 **Ride, Vaquero!**
1953 **East of Sumatra**
1953 **Blowing Wild**
1953 **Cavalleria Rusticana** (aka **Fatal Desire**, 1963)
1953 **Donne Proibite (Angels of Darkness)**
1954 **La Strada**
1954 **The Long Wait**
1954 **Attila**
1954 **The Long Trail** (television)
1955 **The Magnificent Matador**
1955 **The Naked Street**
1955 **Seven Cities of Gold**
1955 **Bandit's Hideout** (television)
1955 **Ulysses**
1956 **Lust for Life** (Academy Award)
1956 **The Man from Del Rio**
1956 **The Wild Party**

1957 **The River's Edge**
1957 **The Ride Back**
1957 **The Hunchback of Notre Dame**
1957 **Wild Is the Wind** (Academy Award nomination)
1958 **Hot Spell**
1958 **The Buccaneer** (director)
1959 **The Black Orchid**
1959 **Warlock**
1959 **Last Train from Gun Hill**
1960 **Heller in Pink Tights**
1960 **Portrait in Black**
1960 **The Savage Innocents**
1960–61 **Becket** (theatre)
1961 **The Guns of Navarone**
1962 **Barabbas**
1962 **Requiem for a Heavyweight**
1962 **Lawrence of Arabia**
1962–63 **Tchin-Tchin** (theatre)
1964 **Behold a Pale Horse**
1964 **The Visit**
1964 **Zorba the Greek** (Academy Award nomination)
1965 **A High Wind in Jamaica**
1965 **Marco the Magnificent**
1966 **Lost Command**
1967 **The Twenty-Fifth Hour**
1967 **The Happening**
1967 **The Rover**
1968 **Guns for San Sebastian**
1968 **The Shoes of the Fisherman**
1968 **The Magus**
1969 **The Secret of Santa Vittoria**
1969 **A Dream of Kings**
1970 **A Walk in the Spring Rain**
1970 **R.P.M.**
1970 **Flap**
1970 **King: A Filmed Record . . . Montgomery to Memphis** (narrator)
1971 **The City** (television)
1971 **The Man and the City** (television series)
1972 **Destiny of a Woman** (television)
1972 **Across 110th Street**
1972 **Arruza** (narrator)
1972 **El Asesinato de Julio César**
1973 **Deaf Smith and Johnny Ears**
1973 **The Don Is Dead**
1974 **The Destructors**
1976 **The Con Artists**
1976 **The Message**
1976 **The Inheritance**
1977 **Jesus of Nazareth** (television)
1977 **Target of an Assassin**
1978 **Children of Sanchez**
1978 **The Greek Tycoon**
1978 **Caravans**
1979 **The Passage**
1980 **Lion of the Desert**
1981 **The Salamander**
1981 **High Risk**
1981 **Crosscurrent**
1982 **Valentina**
1982 **Regina**
1983–86 **Zorba** (theatre)
1987 **Treasure Island** (television)
1988 **A Man of Passion**
1988 **Onassis: The Richest Man in the World** (television)
1989 **Stradivari**
1990 **Revenge**
1990 **The Old Man and the Sea** (television)
1990 **Ghosts Can't Do It**
1991 **Only the Lonely**
1991 **Jungle Fever**
1991 **Mobsters**
1991 **A Star for Two**
1993 **Il Mago (The Magician)** (television)
1993 **Last Action Hero**
1994 **Somebody to Love**
1994 **This Can't Be Love** (television)
1994 **Hercules and the Amazon Women** (television)
1994 **Hercules and the Circle of Fire** (television)
1994 **Hercules and the Lost Kingdom** (television)
1994 **Hercules in the Maze of the Minotaur** (television)
1994 **Hercules in the Underworld** (television)
1995 **A Walk in the Clouds**
1995 **Gotti** (television)
1996 **Seven Servants**
1996 **Il Sindaco (The Mayor)**
1999 **Oriundi**
1999 **Camino de Santiago** (television)
2002 **Avenging Angelo**

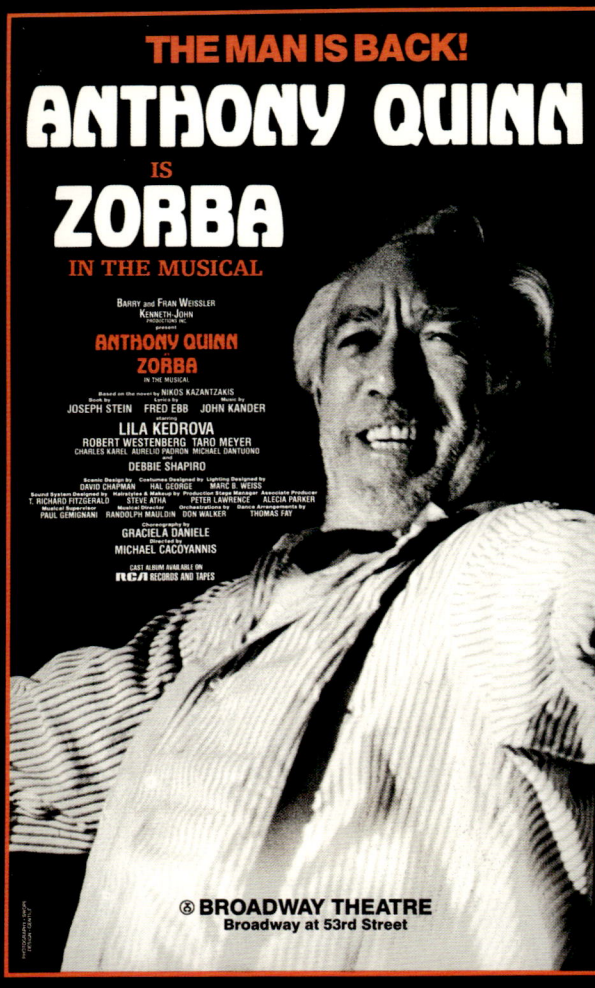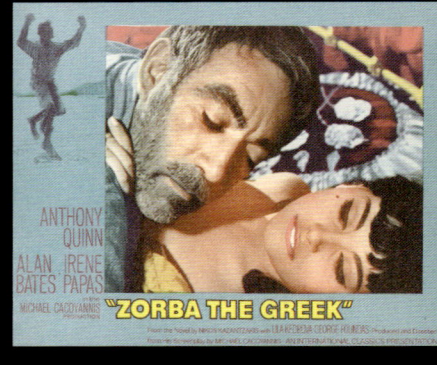

Miscellaneous posters, showcards, and *Playbill*s

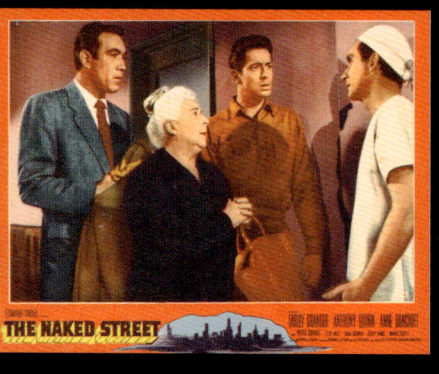  
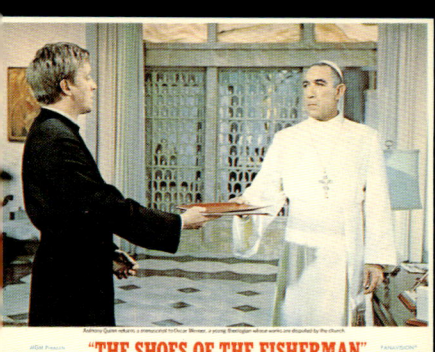  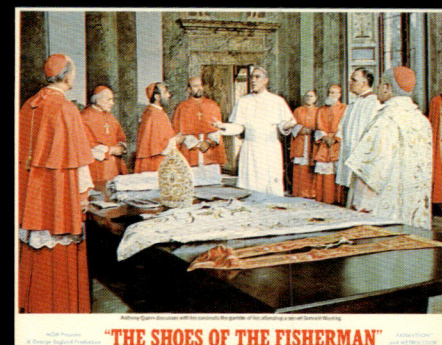
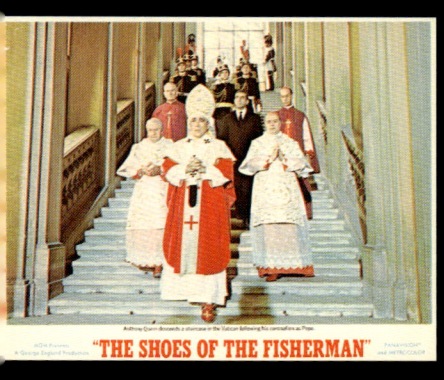 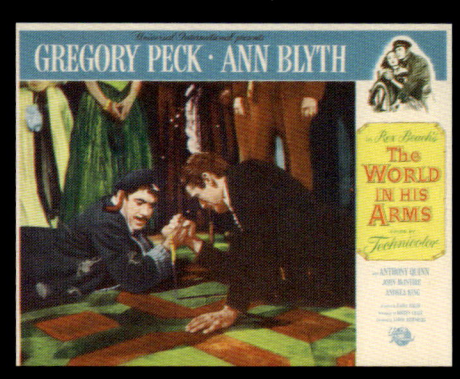 

Anthony's Academy Awards for best supporting actor in *Viva Zapata!* and *Lust for Life* and his 1987 Golden Globe Cecil B. DeMille Award

Photograph Credits

Gen Murakoshi for *Switch* magazine: front cover, 1

Alexander Quinn: 8

Christiane Aleman: 10–11

Aaron Usher: 14–15, 16–17, 53, 60–61, 202–203, 226

Mary Ellen Mark: 19

Sam Shaw/Shaw Family Archives ©: 24 top, 26, 79, 82, 83, 90, 91, 121, 169

Malcolm Grear: 24 bottom, 32, 33, 38, 40, 41, 54–55, 56, 57, 58–59, 62, 63, 64, 65, 66, 67, 72–73, 85, 156, 160–161, 172–173, 177

Olivier Borde/Angeli Agency: 27 top, 29

Karen Philippi: 28, 31, 34–35, 37, 39, 43, 45, 46, 47, 48, 49, 50–51, 68–69, 70, 76–77, 92, 93, 114, 115, 128, 129, 144, 145, 146–147, 148–149, 157, 158–159, 184–185, 199, 201, 204–205, inside back jacket

James Udel, Udel Bros. Studios: 36

© BILD am Sonntag/Peter Timm: 112 top

David Milne-Toronto: 116–117

Albane Navizet/Corbis Outline: 118–119, 186–187, 207

Memo Zack - N.Y.C.: 130–31

Lionello Fabbri: 164, 170–171, 188–189, 190, 191, 192–193, back jacket

Jean-Claude Francolon: 166–167, 196, 197, 211

THIS BOOK WAS DESIGNED
AND SET IN TYPE BY
MALCOLM GREAR DESIGNERS

THE TYPEFACE IS BAUER BODONI AND UNIVERS
THE PAPER IS 115# PARILUX SILK TEXT

EDITED BY EMILY RUSSELL
COPYEDITED BY POLLY WATSON

PRINTED AT MERIDIAN PRINTING
AND BOUND BY BINDTECH INC.

LIMITED EDITION CLAMSHELL CASE
BY PORTFOLIO BOX

LIMITED EDITION RELIEF PRINTS
PRINTED BY LEAH GREAR

SEPTEMBER 2004

UNIQUE COLLECTOR'S EDITION IS AVAILABLE
THROUGH BRISTOL HOUSE PRESS